SCIENCE FUN WITH MUD AND DIRT

Rose Wyler
Pictures by Pat Stewart

JULIAN MESSNER
Published by Simon & Schuster • New York

Text copyright © 1986 by Rose Wyler
Illustrations copyright © 1986 by Pat Stewart

All rights reserved including the right of reproduction in whole or in part in any form.
Published by Julian Messner, a Division of Simon & Schuster, Inc.
Simon & Schuster Building
Rockefeller Center
1230 Avenue of the Americas
New York, New York 10020

Lib. ed.   10 9 8 7 6 5 4 3 2 1

Pbk. ed.   10 9 8 7 6 5 4 3 2 1

JULIAN MESSNER and colophon are trademarks of Simon & Schuster, Inc.
Manufactured in the United States of America

Design by Lisa Hollander

Library of Congress Cataloging in Publication Data
Wyler, Rose. Science fun with mud and dirt.
Summary: Instructions for performing a variety of experiments, indoors and out, with soil.
1. Science—Experiments—Juvenile literature.   (1. Science—Experiments.   2. Experiments)   I. Title. Q164.W84 1986   507'.8
86-8388
ISBN 0-671-55569-3 (lib. bdg.)
ISBN 0-671-62904-2 (pbk.)

FOREWORD

Science is a special kind of knowledge. It explains the world around you and helps you understand how things work.

Ever since early times people have been asking "Why is the sky blue?" or "Why does a seed begin to grow?" or "What is a cloud?" People have always thought and talked about these questions. But you can do something more than that. You can do real science experiments to help you find answers.

This book will show you how to do experiments yourself with mud and dirt. The experiments are easy to set up and are lots of fun. They lead to many exciting discoveries. Try them.

Lewis Love
Great Neck Public Schools
Long Island, New York

ACKNOWLEDGMENTS

The author and publisher wish to thank the people who read the manuscript of this book and made suggestions: Gerald Ames; Lewis Love, Great Neck, New York, Public Schools; Ruth Lindsley, American Museum of Natural History, New York City; and the many young "helpers" who tried the experiments.

Other Books by Rose Wyler

The Giant Golden Book of Astronomy
Prove It!
Secrets in Stones [all written with Gerald Ames]
Real Science Riddles
Science Fun with Peanuts and Popcorn
Science Fun with Toy Boats and Planes

CONTENTS

What Dirt Is Made Of

Dirt is wonderful stuff! It can be gooey, gritty, sticky, or velvety. You can pour it, shape it, build forts and castles, dig tunnels, and grow plants in it. Sometimes it's called soil. It doesn't matter which word you use.

Dirt can be almost any color—red, yellow, brown, black. It can even be pink or white. Yet all dirt is alike in one way. It is made of bits and pieces.

Look at some dirt with a magnifying glass and see the bits and pieces in it. Many kinds may be mixed together. Sort them out, then you can tell what they are.

Try this. Take a quart jar. Fill it half full of dirt and pour in water nearly to the top. Cap the jar. Then shake it twenty times. Let it stand until the dirt settles. It will settle in layers, each one different.

7

How many layers are there? Perhaps you see three: a bottom layer of pebbles, then a layer of coarse grains, then a top layer of fine grains. The water is probably cloudy and has black and brown bits in it.

The next step is to get these things out of the jar.

Try this. Skim off the floating bits with a spoon and spread them on a paper towel. Then slowly pour the water into a smaller jar.

Use the spoon to scoop up the grains in the top layer. Spread them out on another paper towel. Do the same with the grains in the next layer. If there is another layer, dump it on a paper towel.

Now you can find out what is in each layer.

Parts and Particles

Begin with the "floaters." Feel how soft they are! Look at them with a magnifying glass and you see they are bits of wood, leaves, and roots. These bits rot slowly. As they decay, they form black, gooey *humus*.

The other things in soil are hard, stony bits.

The fine grains are *silt*. Hold a coin near your ear, rub some silt on the coin, and you hear a faint sound.

The coarse grains are *sand*. Give them the coin test and they make a louder sound. They scratch the coin too.

Did pieces of stone bigger than sand grains fall to the bottom of the jar? These big pieces are *pebbles*. Some have rough edges, but most of them are round.

Humus, silt, sand, pebbles—what else is in dirt?

Notice the water that's left over. It was clear when you began the experiment. Yet the water is cloudy now. Something from the soil is in the water. But what is it?

Try this. Fold a paper towel in half, then in half again. Lift the front flap of paper toward you to make a cone. Then stick the cone in a funnel that fits a small jar. Pour the water through the paper to strain it.

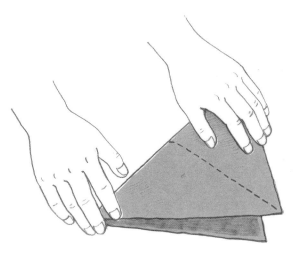

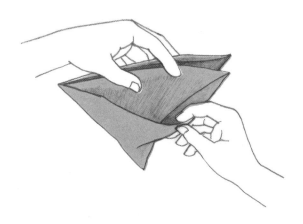

Even after it is strained, the water is cloudy. The particles in it go right through the paper. They are too small to see. But you can tell they are real because the water is cloudy.

Turn a glass upside down. Then spread some of the cloudy water on it. The water dries up, but a film is left. The tiny, tiny particles in this film are *clay*.

So there's one more thing in the soil sample—clay.

Earth Colors

What color is the clay? You can tell by the color of the cloudy water. Most clay is tan or gray, but you can also find clay that is red or yellow.

Examine silt and sand with a magnifying glass and the grains look like tiny gems. You see grains of many colors—black, tan, gray, red, green, purple.

Usually the different colors in dirt blend together. The more humus dirt has in it, the darker its color. Dirt with a lot of red clay in it looks red or pink. But dirt made mainly of white sand looks white.

Kinds of Dirt

To find different kinds of dirt, look in different places—in a garden, in a vacant lot, along a brook, in the woods, and along a road.

Take a sample from each place and put it in a plastic bag or container. Label the dirt in some way so that you know where it came from.

If you look in a place where nothing grows, you probably will find *sand*. Sand has no humus in it. It is clean dirt, made only of stony pieces.

The kind of dirt that makes things dirty contains humus. This kind of dirt is often called soil. Plants can grow in it for many of the things they need are in humus.

You can test soil to find out what kind it is. Just wet a wad of soil. See how it holds together. Then rub the wad against your thumb and feel it.

Sandy soil falls apart easily and feels gritty. It is mostly sand, mixed with a little silt, clay, and humus.

Loam forms clods and feels like velvet. About half of it is sand, a third is clay, and the rest is silt and humus.

Clay soil sticks together and feels greasy. At least half of it is clay; the rest is sand, silt, and humus.

How many kinds of dirt can you find? When you are through testing them, save them for other experiments.

Planting Experiment

You may want to know if plants will grow in all the soils that you find. Plant grass seed in them and see.

Try this. Use paper cups as flower pots. Use a separate cup for each different kind of soil. Punch holes around the bottom of each cup.

Put a half cup of soil in each cup, then plant fifteen grass seeds in each one. Label the cup with the kind of soil that's in it.

Set all the cups on a tray in a warm, sunny place. Pour two tablespoons of water on each one. The extra water will drain through the holes in the cup. Add the same amount of water to each cup every week and watch the grass grow. Which soil has the best crop?

Soil that's sold for lawns and gardens usually is loam. Loam stays moist and has plenty of humus in it. So plants grow well in it. Is that what you find?

Diggers in Dirt

What goes in when the sun shines
But goes out when there's rain?
Look for it on clear days
And you look in vain.

Answer: The earthworm.

Like all animals, earthworms need air. On sunny days there's plenty of air in the soil between the grains. So worms stay in the ground.

16

On rainy days, water soaks into the soil. It forces air out of the spaces between the dirt grains. The worms can't breathe. So up they come.

Try this. Fill a jar with soil. Slowly pour in water and watch for air bubbles. They form as water fills the spaces between the dirt grains.

Try this too. Put a few worms at the bottom of a jar. Pile soil on them. Pour in water and see what the worms do. Don't worry —you won't hurt the worms.

Life Underground

What do earthworms eat? Worms find bits of plants on dirt grains and gulp them down—dirt and all. The dirt is waste and is left on the top of the ground.

As worms cast off dirt they plow the land. They open spaces for plant roots and make air holes. Then the dirt becomes a place where many creatures can eat and breathe.

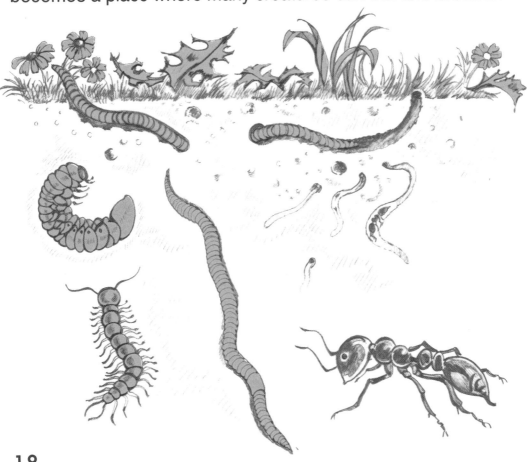

Dig up a shovelful of dirt. Spread it on newspaper and see how many animals are in it. You'll find ants, and maybe a centipede or a millipede.

You'll probably find grubs too. A grub is fat and white and has three pairs of legs. If some other animal doesn't dig the grub up and eat it, it becomes a beetle.

Tunnels and Holes

Who eats grubs? Furry animals with a good sense of smell. The smallest one is the shrew. You never see a shrew because it lives underground. But you may see where it has been.

Shrews mark their way under a lawn by ridges of loose dirt. They push the dirt aside as they dig tunnels and search for insects and worms.

The mole makes the same kind of tunnel. This animal is somewhat bigger than a shrew. Yet it often uses the shrew's tunnel. Many mice do, too.

If you find a ridge in a lawn, look for an opening. That's where digging started. Trace the ridge from there to see how far it goes. The tunnel under it may be a long runway that's used by many unseen animals.

Many holes that you find in woods and in parks lead to animal dens. Some holes are large; others are small. To see how deep a hole is, use a stick. The size of a hole tells something about the animal that made it.

If a hole is just a few inches wide, it may belong to a chipmunk. Its hole is usually hidden by a log. It slants down about three feet, then opens into pockets. Seeds and nuts are stored in some pockets. Others are used to sleep in and to raise young.

The skunk's den is quite big. The skunk sleeps in it by day, then goes out at night. It looks for grubs, digging pits in the grass when it finds them.

The porcupine also stays in a big den until dark. At night it nibbles on twigs and digs for roots.

Don't worry if you find traces of a porcupine or a skunk. Porcupines can't shoot quills, and skunks squirt their smelly spray only when they are in danger.

A digger that may be a pest is the woodchuck or groundhog. It eats plants, and eats a lot, for it's fairly big.

Above ground, the woodchuck's den has three or more holes. All but one are hidden by dirt. That one hole is bare and goes straight down about two feet. A woodchuck often sits there until it sees an enemy. Then, all at once it drops out of sight, down into the hole.

Underground the den has many side rooms. Woodchucks sleep in them at night, and all through the winter. From two to fourteen woodchucks stay in one den during the winter. Sometimes other animals are in the den, too.

Who Goes There?

Animals often use holes made by other animals. Yet if you discover a hole, you may be able to tell who is using it. You can do detective work.

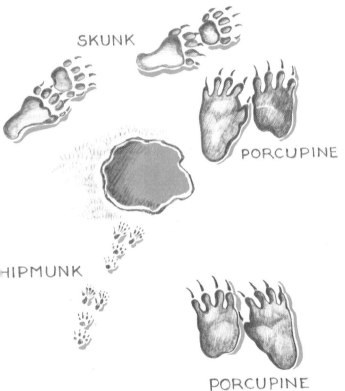

SKUNK

PORCUPINE

CHIPMUNK

PORCUPINE

WOODCHUCK

Try this. Make a ring of mud around the hole. The next day look for footprints in the mud. If there are none, keep up the detective work for a few more nights.

If you find footprints, measure both front and rear tracks. Compare them to pictures of animal tracks. When you find one that matches the mud prints, then you know who lives in the den. The case is closed!

Mud Pie Science

Experiments with mud? Why not? Mud can be poured, spread, and molded. It is a natural plastic, and is very useful.

Bricks and pottery can be shaped from mud. Pavement for roads can be made with it. Houses can be built with it.

How are these things made? What kind of mud is used? How is it mixed? Can you make mud stickier? Experiments with mud pies and puddles will help you find answers.

Puddle Tests

Not all dirt makes mud. You see this after a rain. In some places the dirt is dry. In others the dirt has turned into mud and has puddles in it.

To find out why, experiment with sand and with soils that contain humus. Use dry dirt and see how puddles form.

Try this. You will need a dish for each kind of dirt you are testing. Put two tablespoons of each kind of dirt in a pile on a separate dish. Make a hollow in each pile. Then pour a spoonful of water into it. Watch what happens to the water.

A sand pile drains fast, doesn't it? No puddle forms in it. If you try to make a mud ball from the sand, it falls apart. Meanwhile puddles form in the other piles. The dirt in them gets sticky and makes fine mud balls. As you see, mud and puddles go together.

25

Sand dries quickly. Look at some sand with a magnifying glass and you can see why. The grains are jagged. They do not fit tightly together. Water runs right through the spaces between them. The water doesn't form a puddle and the sand doesn't form mud.

Try digging a hole in sand. The hole soon fills up, unless you pour water in it and wet the sides.

Sand grains stick together only while they are wet. When sand is wet, you can shape it and build with it. Add water as you build and you can make a high sand castle.

The castle will crumble when the sand dries. But then you can build another one.

Dirt with humus stays wet for some time. The humus sops up water like a sponge. The tiny silt grains in the dirt are close together and they keep water from draining. Trapped, the water clings to the clay particles. A puddle forms and the dirt becomes mud.

The water in mud acts like cement. That's why a mud ball holds together when it's wet but crumbles when it's dry.

As mud dries, it usually falls apart. Only a stiff, sticky mixture stays cemented together. That kind of mud can be molded and used in many ways.

27

Baking Mud Pies

Everyone has made mud pies. But have you ever baked one? Baking a pie is a way to test mud. You can see if the mud will hold the shape you give it.

For pie plates, use metal lids from jars. If you need mud, mix up some. Put a tablespoon of dirt in a dish, and add about a teaspoon of water. That will give you enough mud for three small pies.

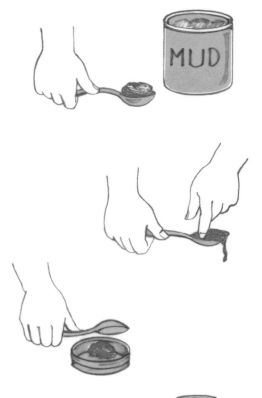

Try this. Fill a teaspoon with mud, then level it off. Turn the spoon upside down and get the mud onto a jar lid. In hot weather, bake the pie in the sun. In cold weather, set it on a hot radiator. Bake the pie until it is dry.

Does the pie stay in shape after it cools?

Stickier Mud

If the pie comes apart, the mud isn't sticky enough. To make it stickier, add some powdered clay. You probably can get powdered clay at school. Or you can get it at a store that sells art supplies.

Mix a quarter-teaspoon of powdered clay with the leftover mud. Then bake a second pie. If it falls apart, add more clay to the mud and bake a third pie. And if that pie isn't firm, use mud made from another kind of dirt.

Try dirt from below the topsoil. The dirt down there usually has no humus in it and contains lots of clay. It makes very sticky mud.

Working with Clay

Beds of nearly pure clay can be found in many places. The clay looks somewhat like rock, for the tiny particles in it are packed close together.

Bits of mineral may be mixed with the particles. Iron rust makes clay red; traces of copper give it a bluish color. If clay is gray, there are bits of black carbon in it.

Clay that's in the ground is called wild clay. Before it is used, the clay is dried, crushed into powder, and strained. Potters who can find wild clay often clean it themselves. Otherwise they buy clay that's ready for use.

You've worked with clay, haven't you? So you know what a great material it is. While it's wet, you can shape it into dishes or dinosaurs or anything you like.

After clay dries, it keeps the shape that it was made into. But it is still soft. It gets harder when it's baked at very high heat. That's why clay pottery is always baked in a special oven called a kiln.

Making pottery is an old art. It began so long ago that no one knows who first learned to use clay.

Perhaps someone noticed puddles with very sticky mud at the bottom and saw that water stayed in them. That led to an idea. Why not use the very sticky mud for pots to hold water? And as it happened, the idea worked.

Perhaps the person who first had that bright idea was a child—someone who liked puddles!

Neat Nest

Have you ever seen a robin's nest? It's a neat, round cup of dried mud. How was it made, you wonder.

The robin starts with straw and twigs. Using its beak, the bird sticks them together with dabs of mud. It stamps down the mud, then packs in more straw. When the mud hardens, new dabs are added and the nest grows. Now the robin works inside, turning in circles. It shapes the mud with its body and the nest becomes a big cup.

Just for fun, pretend you're a robin. Try to make a nest out of mud. Can you make one that doesn't crack?

32

As mud dries, it shrinks. If some parts dry faster than others, they shrink faster. Then the mud cracks.

Cracking can be prevented. One way to do this is to add straw to mud. The straw soaks up water and keeps it from collecting in spots. Then the mud dries evenly.

Test some mud and straw and see for yourself.

Try this. Take two large jar lids. Fill one with plain mud. Fill the other with mud and bits of straw. Dry them side by side. Probably the plain mud cracks while the mud with straw holds together. If it doesn't, try a mixture with more straw.

Now you see why a robin's nest doesn't crack. The robin always adds straw to mud. Lots of other birds also use mud for their nests.

Building a Mud House

The first houses in the world were probably mud houses. In some places, people still build them.

A mud house can be built from just a few things—sticks, grass, mud mixed with straw. The frame is quickly made. Some of the sticks are set upright. Others are set crosswise and tied in place with grass.

Working from the ground up, mud is packed between the sticks. When one layer dries, another is added until there's a high wall. A roof that's made of grass or big leaves is put on top, and the house is ready.

Could you make a mud house? Try making a model of one. You'll find it takes a lot of skill to build with mud.

Sun-dried Bricks

If you live where it is hot and dry, you know what adobe is. Adobe is a mud mixture that is very stiff. Bricks are molded from it, then dried in the sun.

If rain doesn't get at the bricks, they last a very long time. Some adobe houses that are now in use were built centuries ago. That's why people still build with adobe and make it in the same old way.

The adobe is mixed in a large vat. The dirt used is loam, for it contains both sand and clay. Water and straw are added to it until the mixture is fairly stiff. Then some mud is slapped on a tilted shovel to see if it slides off. If it sticks, sand or more straw is added.

When the mixture is just right, it is poured into a big mold. This is a frame with dividers for the bricks.

The next step is drying the adobe. After ten days, a brick is tested by dropping it. If the brick breaks, more drying is needed. If it doesn't break, the adobe is hard and firm. Now building can begin.

When the house is finished, it is coated with plaster. The plaster keeps the adobe dry. It looks nice, too.

Homemade Adobe

You can make adobe anywhere, if you work indoors. You can build a house with it too—a small house, that is.

Try this. Mix two cups of loam with water. Then add bits of straw and sand until you get a stiff mud.

For the mold, use an ice cube tray with dividers. Pour the mud into the tray and dry it in a warm place. After ten days, take out a brick and drop it to test it. If the brick breaks, the adobe is still moist. Dry it until it passes the drop test. Then start your building.

Are any bricks left? If you have an extra one, soak it in a bowl. The water soon clouds up with particles of clay. The brick is coming apart!

No wonder adobe houses are coated with plaster.

Turning Mud into Stone

If you soak pieces of red brick, the water stays clear. This kind of brick doesn't fall apart the way adobe does. Yet it, too, is made from a mud mixture.

Notice that the brick has pebbles in it, along with grains of sand. The red part is clay. Bricks are shaped from this mixture, then baked in very hot ovens. Heat changes the clay, turning mud into stone.

Mud with cement in it hardens in a different way. Cement is a powder made from limestone and clay. Sand and water are added to it to form a stiff mud. Then the mud is spread—maybe on bricks in a wall or on a sidewalk. As the mud dries, air changes it to stone.

Still harder stone is made by adding gravel to sand, cement, and water. This sloshy mud becomes concrete.

Have you ever seen workers mix concrete? They cast it into bricks that look like the ones made of adobe.

For big jobs, concrete is mixed in an iron barrel on a truck. The barrel turns and rattles as the truck takes the concrete to where it is needed. Then the barrel is tipped and the wet mixture is poured.

When used to pave a road, concrete is poured over steel mesh. The steel makes it extra strong.

Concrete for tall buildings is cast around steel rods or bars. It is cast in slabs, layer after layer, as the building is going up.

Rich Soil, Poor Soil

Walk in the woods, or in a park, and you walk on a soft rug of dead leaves. What a wonderful crunching, scrunching sound they make.

Just how thick are the leaves? Kick some aside until you come to dirt. You'll find less than a foot of leaves. Yet year after year, trees lose their leaves. Why don't the leaves pile up, you wonder. Where do they go?

Bacteria and molds, like those that grow on fruit and bread, make leaves rot. Rotting goes on for a year or two until there is nothing left of the leaves. Black, gooey humus forms from them and becomes part of the soil.

Dig up some leaves near the dirt and look on the underside for leaf molds. Some of them form long, white threads. Others are tangled and spread out like cobwebs.

Molds grow in dead logs, too, along with mushrooms and other fungus plants. The fungus plants get food from wood. Then the wood becomes soft and rotten.

Wood rots very slowly—so slowly that you can find lots of stumps older than you. After many years wood is changed into humus. Finally it disappears, just as leaves do. But life in the forest goes on, for humus keeps the soil rich and healthy.

Up Above and
Down Below

Humus forms wherever plants grow. It collects under leaves and becomes part of the *topsoil*.

Topsoil may be sandy soil, or clay soil, or loam. Whichever it is, topsoil is rich because of the humus in it. Humus contains the foods and water that plants need. So topsoil is where seeds sprout and plants grow.

If you look along a stream bank, a new roadcut, or a big, deep hole, you can see how far down the topsoil goes. Topsoil forms a dark layer. In some places it goes down a few inches; in others, it is a few feet thick. Plant roots run all through it.

The soil below is light colored for it lacks humus. It is poor soil with very few plant roots growing in it.

Raindrop Splash

Topsoil and plants need each other. When land is bare, rain hurts the soil. During a storm, drops hit the earth like little bombs. They smash clods of soil and splash the dirt around.

If ground is covered with plants, raindrops strike leaves. Their fall is broken and there is little splash. The topsoil stays in place.

Try this. Shove a pencil through a piece of paper about five inches long. Then plant the pencil in a pot of bare dirt so the paper is slightly above it. Put another pencil and paper in a pot with plants growing in the dirt.

Set both pots outside on a windowsill during a storm. While you stay in the house, watch the raindrops strike. See how much dirt is splashed on each paper.

Rills and Hills

Do you ever watch little streams of rainwater run downhill? They meet, making big streams. If the streams go over bare land, they get muddier and muddier. They wash away soil and cut gullies into the earth.

Plants can prevent this, for roots soak up water. Start a little rainstorm and you'll see that plants hold down soil.

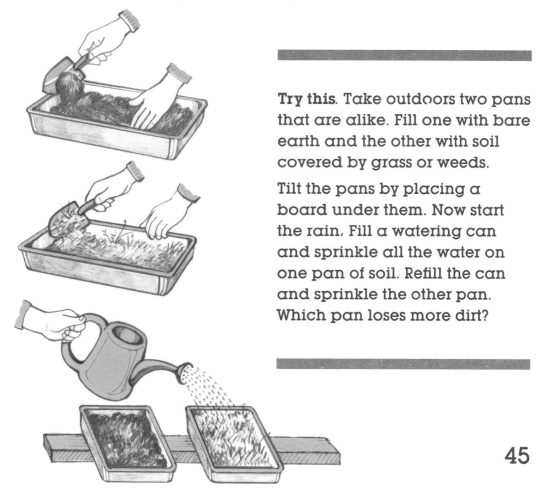

Try this. Take outdoors two pans that are alike. Fill one with bare earth and the other with soil covered by grass or weeds.

Tilt the pans by placing a board under them. Now start the rain. Fill a watering can and sprinkle all the water on one pan of soil. Refill the can and sprinkle the other pan. Which pan loses more dirt?

Dams to Save Soil

Sometimes after a heavy rain, water rushes downhill faster than plants can soak it up. Gullies start to form.

Dams hold back water. But can dams be built quickly to keep gullies from growing? As you know, beavers build dams with branches. Would that kind of dam work?

Try this. Go out again with the two pans that are alike and fill them with dirt. Tilt the pans. Then sprinkle each one with the same amount of water, to make gullies form in them.

In one pan build dams of twigs across a few gullies. Sprinkle both pans with the same amount of water. Is there any difference in the gullies in the two pans?

Do you find that the twig dams work?

You Can Help

Perhaps you can use what you learn. Are there gullies near your house or school? When you see gullies start, get friends to help you keep them from growing.

Gullies are ugly. If you build dams to stop them, you will make the land look better. By putting science to work, you will help save the soil.

Wonderful dirt—how much you have found out about it! What soil is made of, how animals live in it, and how plants grow in it. How bricks and how pots are made. How soil can be harmed, and how it can be saved.

Are there more experiments you can do with dirt? Of course! Try out some of your own ideas, and go right on having science fun with mud and dirt.

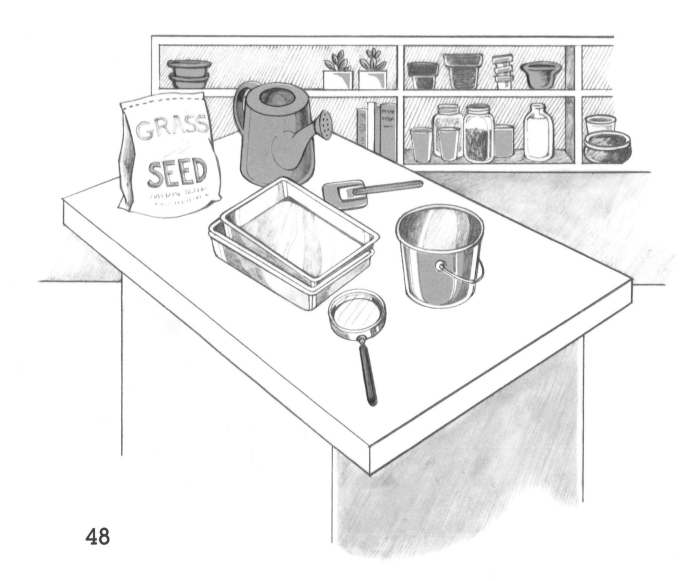